A PACEMAKER® CLASSIC

The Importance of Being Earnest

Oscar Wilde

Abridged and adapted by Sandra Widener

Illustrated by Dennis Dittrich

Upper Saddle River, New Jersey
www.globefearon.com

Project Editor: David Cutts
Lead Editor: Alisa Brightman
Production Editor: Amy Benefiel
Marketing Manager: Kate Krimsky
Art Supervision: Angel Weyant, Eileen Peters
Art Coordinator: Cindy Talocci
Electronic Page Production: Leslie Greenberg
Lissette J. Quiñones, Wanda Rockwell
Manufacturing Supervisor: Mark Cirillo
Cover and Interior Illustrator: Dennis Dittrich

Printed in the United States of America
1 2 3 4 5 6 7 8 9 10   04 03 02 01 00

ISBN: 0-130-23702-7

1-800-848-9500
www.globefearon.com

Contents

Cast of Characters

JOHN WORTHING — Also called Jack, of the Manor House, Woolton, Hertfordshire; he is guardian of Cecily Cardew

ALGERNON MONCRIEFF — Jack's friend

LADY BRACKNELL (AUNT AUGUSTA) — Algernon's aunt and Gwendolen's mother

GWENDOLEN FAIRFAX — Lady Bracknell's daughter

CECILY CARDEW — Jack Worthing's ward (He is her guardian.)

MISS PRISM — Cecily's governess

THE REVEREND CANON CHASUBLE — The pastor of Woolton

LANE — A servant to Algernon

MERRIMAN — The butler at Jack Worthing's Manor House

The Scenes

The action takes place in London and at a country house in Hertfordshire during the 1890s.

ACT I — The living room in Algernon Moncrieff's apartment in London. It is teatime on a summer afternoon

ACT II — The garden at the Manor House, Woolton, the following afternoon

ACT III — The living room at the Manor House, Woolton, immediately following

Act 1

The living room in ALGERNON MONCRIEFF'S *apartment in London. The room is richly decorated. The sound of a piano is heard in the next room.* LANE *is placing afternoon tea on the table. The music stops.* ALGERNON *enters.*

ALGERNON: Did you hear what I was playing, Lane?

LANE: I didn't think it polite to listen, sir.

ALGERNON: I'm sorry for that, for your sake. I don't play well—anyone can play well—but I play with feeling. As far as the piano goes, feeling is my gift.

LANE: Yes, sir.

ALGERNON: Have you made the cucumber sandwiches for Lady Bracknell?

LANE: Yes, sir. (*hands them on a platter*)

ALGERNON (*looks at them, takes two, and sits down on the sofa*)*:* By the way, Lane, I was looking at your records. On Thursday night, Lord Shoreman and Mr. Worthing dined with me. They had eight bottles of champagne?

LANE: Yes, sir. Eight bottles and a pint.

ALGERNON: Why is it that in a bachelor's house the servants always drink the champagne? I ask only to know.

LANE: I think it is because the wine is better, sir. I have noticed that in married households the champagne is rarely that good.

ALGERNON: Good heavens! Is marriage so bad as that?

LANE: I believe it *is* very pleasant sir. I have had very little experience with it myself up to now. I have only been married once. That was quite a mistake.

ALGERNON (*lazily*): I am not much interested in your family life, Lane.

LANE: No, sir. It is not very interesting. I never think of it myself.

ALGERNON: Very natural, I am sure. That will do, Lane. Thank you.

LANE: Thank you, sir.

(LANE *goes out.*)

ALGERNON: Lane's views on marriage seem a bit careless. Really, if the servants don't set a good example for us, what is the use of them? They seem to have no sense of morals.

(LANE *enters.*)

LANE (*announcing a visitor*): Mr. Ernest Worthing.

(JACK [JOHN WORTHING] *enters. He hands his top hat and cane to* LANE. *The servant takes them and goes out.*)

ALGERNON: How are you, my dear Ernest? What brings you to town?

JACK: Oh, pleasure, pleasure! What else should bring one anywhere? Eating as usual, I see, Algy!

ALGERNON (*stiffly*): I believe most people eat a bit at 5:00 P.M. Where have you been since last Thursday?

JACK (*sitting on the sofa*): In the country.

ALGERNON: What on Earth do you do there?

JACK (*pulling off his gloves*): When I am in town, I amuse myself. When I am in the country, I amuse others. It is very boring.

ALGERNON: Who do you amuse?

JACK (*airily*): Oh, neighbors, neighbors.

ALGERNON: Got nice neighbors in your part of Shropshire?

JACK: Perfectly awful. Never speak to them.

ALGERNON: How much you must amuse them! (*goes over and takes a sandwich*) By the way, Shropshire is where you live, is it not?

JACK: Eh? Shropshire? Yes, of course. Hallo! Why all these cups? Why sandwiches? Who is coming to tea?

ALGERNON: Oh! Just Aunt Augusta and Gwendolen.

JACK: How delightful!

ALGERNON: Yes, that is all very well. Aunt Augusta won't like your being here, though.

JACK: May I ask why?

ALGERNON: My dear fellow, the way you flirt with Gwendolen is terrible. It is almost as bad as the way Gwendolen flirts with you.

JACK (*while staring at a sandwich*): I am in love with Gwendolen. I have come to town just to ask her to marry me.

ALGERNON: I thought you had come for pleasure. I call that business.

JACK: How unromantic you are!

ALGERNON: I really don't see anything romantic in asking someone to marry you. It is romantic to be in love. Yet, there is nothing romantic about a proposal. Why, it may be accepted. It often is. Then, the excitement is all over. If I ever do get married, I will try to forget that I am married.

JACK: I am sure of that, dear Algy. The Divorce Court was made for people who think like you.

ALGERNON: Oh! There is no use thinking about that. Divorces are made in heaven. (JACK *puts out his hand to take a sandwich.* ALGERNON *stops him*) Please don't touch the cucumber sandwiches. They were ordered just for Aunt Augusta. (*takes one and eats it*)

JACK: Well, you are eating them.

ALGERNON: That is different. She is *my* aunt. (*takes the plate*) Have some bread and butter. The bread and butter is for Gwendolen. She likes it very much.

JACK (*moving to the table and helping himself*): Very good bread and butter it is, too.

ALGERNON: Well, you do not need to eat it all. You are not married to her. I don't think you ever will be.

JACK: Why do you say that?

ALGERNON: Well, in the first place, girls never marry the men they flirt with. Girls don't think it's right to do so.

JACK: Oh, that is nonsense!

ALGERNON: It isn't. It is the truth. It explains the large number of single men one sees. In the second place, I don't give my permission.

JACK: Your permission!

ALGERNON: My dear fellow, Gwendolen is my cousin. Before I allow you to marry her, you will have to explain to me who Cecily is. (*rings bell*)

JACK: Cecily! What do you mean? I don't know anyone named Cecily.

(LANE *enters.*)

ALGERNON: Bring me that cigarette case that Mr. Worthing left the last time he was here.

LANE: Yes, sir. (*He goes out.*)

JACK: Have you had my cigarette case all this time? I wish you had let me know.

(LANE *enters with the cigarette case on a platter.* ALGERNON *takes it.* LANE *goes out.*)

ALGERNON (*opens case and looks at it*): Now that I look at it, I see that the case isn't yours after all.

JACK: Of course it's mine. (*moving to him*) You have seen me with it a hundred times. You have no right to read what is written inside.

ALGERNON: Oh! There should be no set rule about what one shouldn't read. More than half of modern life is based on what one shouldn't read.

JACK: I know that. I do not want to talk about modern life. It isn't the sort of thing one should talk of in private. I just want my cigarette case back.

ALGERNON: Yes, but this isn't yours, after all. This is a present from someone named Cecily. You said you did not know anyone by that name.

JACK: Well, if you must know, Cecily is my aunt.

ALGERNON: Your aunt!

JACK: Yes, charming old lady she is, too. Just give it back to me, Algy.

ALGERNON (*moving to the back of the sofa*): Why does she call herself little Cecily if she is your aunt? (*reading*) "From little Cecily with her fondest love."

JACK (*moving to the sofa and kneeling upon it*): That means nothing. Some aunts are tall. Some aunts are not tall. That is a matter that surely an aunt can choose for herself. Now, give me back my cigarette case. (*follows* ALGERNON *around the room*)

ALGERNON: Yes. However, why does your aunt call you her uncle? "From little Cecily, with fondest love to her dear Uncle Jack." An aunt may be small. Why, though, should an aunt call her own nephew her uncle? Besides, your name isn't Jack. It is Ernest.

JACK: It isn't Ernest. It's Jack.

ALGERNON: You have always told me it was Ernest. I have told everyone you are Ernest. You answer to the name of Ernest. You are the most earnest looking person I ever saw. The name Ernest is on your calling cards. Here is one of them. (*taking it from the case*) "Mr. Ernest Worthing, B4, The Albany." I'll keep this as proof that your name is Ernest if ever you try to deny it to me, or to Gwendolen, or to anyone else. (*puts the card in his pocket*)

JACK: Well, my name is Ernest in town and Jack in the country. The cigarette case was given to me in the country.

ALGERNON: That does not explain why your small Aunt Cecily calls you her dear uncle. Come, old boy, you had better explain. Tell me the whole story. I must say that I have always thought you were a secret Bunburyist. I am quite sure of it now.

JACK: Bunburyist? What do you mean by that?

ALGERNON: I'll tell you what that means. First, though, tell me why you are Ernest in town and Jack in the country.

7

JACK: Give me my cigarette case first.

ALGERNON: Here it is. (*hands him the cigarette case*) Now, tell me.

JACK: What I have to say is very ordinary. Old Mr. Thomas Cardew adopted me when I was a baby. He made me guardian to his granddaughter, Miss Cecily Cardew. Cecily calls me her uncle out of respect. That is something you would not understand. She lives at my house in the country. Her governess, Miss Prism, cares for her.

ALGERNON: Where is that place in the country?

JACK: It does not matter to you, dear boy. You are not going to be invited. I can tell you it is not in Shropshire, however.

ALGERNON: I thought so. I have Bunburyed all over Shropshire. I never saw your house. Now, go on. Why are you Ernest in town and Jack in the country?

JACK: My dear Algy, I do not think you can understand why. You are not serious enough. A person who is a guardian needs to be very upright. Being upright, though, does not lead to much health or happiness. So, as an excuse to go to town, I have always said I had a younger brother named Ernest. He gets into the most awful trouble. That, my dear Algy, is the truth, pure and simple.

ALGERNON: The truth is rarely pure and never simple. Modern life would be very dull if it were. I now know, however, that you are a Bunburyist. You are one of the best.

JACK: What do you mean?

ALGERNON: You have made up a very useful younger brother called Ernest. To help this brother, you come up to town as often as you like. I have made up a useful friend named Bunbury. He is always ill. That allows me to go to the country when I wish. Bunbury is very valuable. If it wasn't for his very bad health, I wouldn't be able to dine with you tonight. Last week, I told Aunt Augusta I would go to her house.

JACK: I haven't asked you to dine with me tonight.

ALGERNON: I know. You are careless about sending out invitations. Nothing annoys people more than not receiving invitations.

JACK: You should dine with your Aunt Augusta.

ALGERNON: I will not. To begin with, I dined there on Monday. Once a week is enough. In the second place, when I do dine there, I am always treated as a member of the family. In the third place, I know she will seat me next to Mary Farquhar. Mary always flirts with her own husband at dinner. The number of women in London who flirt with their own husbands is shocking. It looks so bad. It is just washing one's clean linen in public. Besides, now I know you are

10

a real Bunburyist. I want to talk to you about Bunburying. I want to tell you the rules.

JACK: I'm not a Bunburyist at all. If Gwendolen will marry me, I am going to kill my brother. Indeed, I think I'll kill him in any case. Cecily is too interested in him. I think you should do the same with your ill friend with the odd name.

ALGERNON: I will not part with Bunbury. If you ever get married, you will be glad you have a Bunbury. A man who marries without a Bunbury has a hard time.

JACK: That is silly. Gwendolen is the only girl I ever wanted to marry. If I do, I will not want Bunbury.

ALGERNON: Then, your wife will. In married life, three is company, and two is none.

JACK: For heaven's sake, don't be so doubtful. It's so easy to be doubtful.

ALGERNON: My dear fellow, it isn't easy to be anything these days. There's so much competition about. (*The sound of an electric bell is heard.*) Ah! That must be Aunt Augusta. Only relatives, or shopkeepers wanting their money, ever ring in that serious way. Now, let's say I can get her out of the way for ten minutes. Then, you can ask Gwendolen to marry you. Then, may I dine with you tonight?

JACK: I suppose so, if you want to.

ALGERNON: Yes, but you must be serious about it. I hate people who are not serious about meals. It is so shallow of them.

(LANE *enters*.)

LANE (*announcing visitors*): Lady Bracknell and Miss Fairfax.

(LADY BRACKNELL *and* GWENDOLEN *enter.* ALGERNON *meets them.*)

LADY BRACKNELL: Good afternoon, dear Algernon. I hope you are behaving very well.

ALGERNON: I'm feeling very well, Aunt Augusta.

LADY BRACKNELL: That's not the same thing. In fact, the two things rarely go together. (*sees* JACK *and greets him coldly*)

ALGERNON (*to* GWENDOLEN): You look lovely!

GWENDOLEN: I am always lovely! Aren't I, Mr. Worthing?

JACK: You're perfect, Miss Fairfax.

GWENDOLEN: Oh! I hope I am not that. It would leave no room for changes. I plan to change in many ways. (GWENDOLEN *and* JACK *sit down together in the corner of the room.*)

LADY BRACKNELL: I'm sorry if we are a little late, Algernon. I had to call on dear Lady Harbury. I hadn't been there since her poor husband's death. I never saw a woman so changed. She looks 20 years younger. Now, I'll have a cup of tea and one of those nice cucumber sandwiches you promised me.

13

ALGERNON: Certainly, Aunt Augusta. (*goes over to the tea table*)

LADY BRACKNELL (*sitting herself on the sofa*): Won't you come and sit here, Gwendolen?

GWENDOLEN: Thanks, Mamma, I'm quite comfortable where I am.

ALGERNON (*picking up the empty plate in horror*): Good heavens! Lane! Why are there no cucumber sandwiches? I ordered them specially.

LANE (*gravely*): There were no cucumbers in the market this morning, sir. I went down twice.

ALGERNON: No cucumbers!

LANE: No, sir.

ALGERNON: That will do, Lane. Thank you.

LANE: Thank you, sir. (*He goes out.*)

ALGERNON: I am very sad, Aunt Augusta, about there being no cucumbers.

LADY BRACKNELL: It does not matter, Algernon. I had some crumpets with Lady Harbury. She seems to be living just for pleasure now.

ALGERNON: I hear her hair has turned quite gold from grief.

LADY BRACKNELL: It certainly has changed its color. As to why, I cannot say. (ALGERNON *hands her tea.*) Thank you. I've quite a treat for you tonight, Algernon. I am going to seat you next to Mary Farquhar. She is such a nice woman and so kind to her husband. It's delightful to watch them.

ALGERNON: I am afraid, Aunt Augusta, I shall not be able to dine with you tonight after all.

LADY BRACKNELL (*frowning*): If you do not come, the seating will have to be changed. Your uncle will have to dine upstairs. Fortunately, he is used to that.

ALGERNON: It is a great bore and a disappointment. However, I have just had a telegram. My poor friend Bunbury is very ill again. (*exchanges looks with* JACK) They think I should be with him.

LADY BRACKNELL: It is very strange. This Mr. Bunbury suffers from curiously bad health.

ALGERNON: Yes, poor Bunbury is often ill.

LADY BRACKNELL: Well, it is high time Mr. Bunbury made up his mind whether to live or die. This back and forth with the question will not do. I do not think this sympathy with the sick is a good idea. I consider it gloomy. Illness is not a thing to be encouraged. I should be grateful if you would ask Mr. Bunbury to be kind enough not to be ill on Saturday. I need you to arrange my music. It is my last party. One has to do something to aid conversation. This is very true at this time of year. Everyone has said whatever he or she had to say. In most cases, it was not much.

ALGERNON: I'll speak to Bunbury, Aunt Augusta, if he is still conscious. I think he'll be fine by Saturday. You see, if one plays good music, people don't listen. If one plays bad music, they don't talk. I'll show you the songs I've chosen. Will you please come into the next room?

LADY BRACKNELL: Thank you, Algernon. That is very kind. (*rising and following* ALGERNON) I'm sure the songs will be delightful. Of course, I cannot allow French songs. People always seem to think they are not proper. They either look shocked, which is rude, or they laugh, which is worse. Gwendolen, you will come with me.

GWENDOLEN: Certainly, Mamma. (LADY BRACKNELL *and* ALGERNON *go into the music room.* GWENDOLEN *stays behind.*)

JACK: Lovely day it has been, Miss Fairfax.

GWENDOLEN: Please do not talk to me about the weather, Mr. Worthing. When people do, I always feel quite sure that they mean something else. That makes me nervous.

JACK: I do mean something else.

GWENDOLEN: I thought so. In fact, I am never wrong.

JACK: While Lady Bracknell is gone, I should like to...

GWENDOLEN: Yes, you should. Mamma has a way of coming back quickly into a room. I have had to speak to her about that.

JACK (*nervously*): Miss Fairfax, ever since I met you I have admired you more than any girl . . . I have ever met since. . . I met you.

GWENDOLEN: Yes, I know that. I wish that in public you had been more friendly. I have always been interested in you. Even before I met you I liked you. (JACK *looks at her in amazement.*) We live, Mr. Worthing, in an age of ideals. The better monthly magazines say so. My ideal has always been to love someone named Ernest. There is something in that name. It inspires confidence. When Algernon told me he had a friend named Ernest, I knew I would love you.

JACK: You really love me, Gwendolen?

GWENDOLEN (*coolly*): With fiery love!

JACK: Darling! You don't know how happy you've made me.

GWENDOLEN: My own dear Ernest!

JACK: Do you mean that you could not love me if my name wasn't Ernest?

GWENDOLEN: Your name is Ernest.

JACK: Yes, I know it is. What if my name was something else? You couldn't love me then?

GWENDOLEN (*smoothly*): Ah! That is not the case, so it does not matter.

JACK: Darling, I don't much care for the name of Ernest. The name does not suit me well at all.

GWENDOLEN: It suits you perfectly. It is a wonderful name. It has a music of its own.

JACK: Well, really, Gwendolen, I do think there are much nicer names. Jack, for example.

GWENDOLEN: Jack? No, there is very little music in the name Jack. It does not thrill. It makes no vibrations. I have known several Jacks. They were all plain. The only really safe name is Ernest.

JACK: Gwendolen, I must be christened at once—I mean, we must marry at once. There is no time to be lost.

GWENDOLEN: Married, Mr. Worthing?

JACK: (*astounded*): Well...yes. You know that I love you. You led me to think, Miss Fairfax, that you feel the same.

GWENDOLEN: I adore you. However, you haven't asked me to marry you. Nothing has been said at all about marriage. The subject has not been touched on.

JACK: May I ask you to marry me now?

GWENDOLEN: I think it would be an excellent time. Mr. Worthing, I think it only fair to tell you that I have decided to marry you.

JACK: Gwendolen!

GWENDOLEN: Yes, Mr. Worthing. What have you got to say to me?

JACK: You know what I have to say to you.

GWENDOLEN: Yes, but you haven't said it.

JACK: Gwendolen, will you marry me? (*goes on his knees*)

GWENDOLEN: Of course I will, darling. How long it took you to ask! I am afraid you have had very little experience in how to propose.

JACK: My own one, I have never loved anyone in the world but you.

GWENDOLEN: Yes, but men often propose for practice. My brother Gerald does. All of my girlfriends tell me so. What blue eyes you have, Ernest! I hope you will always look at me like that, especially when other people are around.

(LADY BRACKNELL *enters.*)

LADY BRACKNELL (*in a thundering voice*): Mr. Worthing! Rise, sir, from this awkward position! It is most impolite.

GWENDOLEN: Mamma! (JACK *tries to rise; she holds him back.*) I must ask you to leave. This is no place for you. Besides, Mr. Worthing has not finished.

LADY BRACKNELL: Finished what, may I ask?

GWENDOLEN: I am engaged to Mr. Worthing, Mamma. (GWENDOLEN *and* JACK *rise together.*)

LADY BRACKNELL: Excuse me. You are not engaged to anyone. When you are engaged, either your father or I will tell you so. An engagement should be a surprise. It is not a matter that a young girl should arrange. Now, I have a few questions for you, Mr. Worthing. You, Gwendolen, will wait for me in the carriage.

GWENDOLEN (*with disapproval*): Mamma!

LADY BRACKNELL: In the carriage, Gwendolen! (GWENDOLEN *goes to the door. She and* JACK *blow kisses to each other behind* LADY BRACKNELL'S *back.* LADY BRACKNELL *looks about as if she cannot understand what the noise is. She finally turns around.*) Gwendolen, the carriage!

GWENDOLEN: Yes, Mamma. (*She goes out, looking back at* JACK.)

LADY BRACKNELL (*sitting down*): You can take a seat, Mr. Worthing. (*looks in her pocket for a notebook and pencil*)

JACK: Thank you, Lady Bracknell. I would like to stand.

LADY BRACKNELL (*pencil and notebook in hand*): I must tell you that you are not on my list of suitable young men. I have the same list as the dear Duchess of Bolton. We work together. However, I will enter your name, if your answers are what a loving mother wants to hear. Do you smoke?

JACK: Well, yes, I do.

LADY BRACKNELL: I am glad to hear it. A man should always have a hobby. There are far too many men doing nothing in London as it is. How old are you?

JACK: Twenty-nine.

LADY BRACKNELL: A very good age to be married at. A man who wants to get married should know either everything or nothing. Which do you know?

JACK (*after some hesitation*): I know nothing, Lady Bracknell.

LADY BRACKNELL: I am glad to hear it. I do not like anything that gets in the way of a natural lack of knowledge. Modern education is unsound. Luckily, in England, education has no effect. If it did, it would be a serious danger to the upper classes. It might lead to violence. Is your income from land or investments?

JACK: From investments, mostly.

LADY BRACKNELL: That is fine.

JACK: I have a country house with some land, of course. It is about 1,500 acres, I believe. That is not my real income. As far as I can tell, those who hunt on my land without my permission are the only ones who make anything from it.

LADY BRACKNELL: A country house! How many bedrooms? Well, that point can be cleared up later. You have a house in town, I hope? Gwendolen is a simple, unspoiled girl. She could not be expected to live in the country.

JACK: Well, I own a house in Belgrave Square in London. It is rented by the year to Lady Bloxham. I can get it back whenever I like, at six months' notice.

LADY BRACKNELL: Lady Bloxham? I don't know her.

JACK: Oh, she goes out very little. She is a much older lady.

LADY BRACKNELL: Ah, today that may not mean someone is respectable. What number in Belgrave Square?

JACK: 149.

LADY BRACKNELL (*shaking her head*): The unfashionable side. Well, that can be fixed.

JACK: Do you mean the fashion, or the side?

LADY BRACKNELL (*sternly*): Both, if necessary. What are your politics?

JACK: Well, I am afraid I really have none.

LADY BRACKNELL: That is fine. Now, to lesser matters. Are your parents living?

JACK: I have lost both my parents.

LADY BRACKNELL: Both? That seems careless. Who was your father? He was, it seems, a man of some wealth. Was he born of the upper classes?

JACK: I really don't know. The fact is, Lady Bracknell, I said I had lost my parents. It would be nearer the truth to say that my parents seem to have lost me. I don't know who I am by birth. I was...well, I was found.

LADY BRACKNELL: Found!

JACK: The late Mr. Thomas Cardew, a kind old gentleman, found me. He gave me the name of Worthing. He happened to have a ticket for Worthing in his pocket. Worthing is a place in Sussex. It is a seaside resort.

LADY BRACKNELL: Where did the kind gentleman who had a ticket for this seaside resort find you?

JACK (*seriously*): In a handbag.

LADY BRACKNELL: A handbag?

JACK (*very seriously*): Yes, Lady Bracknell. I was found in a handbag. It was a large, black leather handbag. It had handles on it. An ordinary handbag, in fact.

LADY BRACKNELL: Where did this Mr. Cardew come across this ordinary handbag with the handles?

JACK: In the coat room at Victoria Station. It was given to him by mistake instead of his own bag.

LADY BRACKNELL: The coat room at Victoria Station?

JACK: Yes. The Brighton line.

LADY BRACKNELL: The line is not important. (*grandly, as if delivering a speech*) Mr. Worthing, I am confused by what you have just told me. To have been born in a handbag, whether or not it has handles, shows no respect for family life. A coat room in a railway station is hardly a good start for a place in high society.

JACK: What should I do? I would do anything to make Gwendolen happy.

LADY BRACKNELL: I would tell you, Mr. Worthing, to find some relatives as soon as possible. Make an effort to find at least one parent before the season is over.

JACK: I don't see how I can do that. I can show you the handbag. It is at home. I think that should satisfy you, Lady Bracknell.

LADY BRACKNELL (*as though thinking about a horror*): Me, sir! What has it to do with me? Lord Bracknell and I would not dream of allowing our only daughter to marry into a coat room! Good morning, Mr. Worthing! (LADY BRACKNELL *sweeps out royally.*)

JACK: Good morning! (ALGERNON *is in the other room. He strikes up the Wedding March.* JACK *looks furious and goes to the door.*) Don't play that horrible tune, Algy! How idiotic you are! (*The music stops, and* ALGERNON *enters cheerily.*)

ALGERNON: Didn't it go well, old boy? Did Gwendolen say no? It is the way she is.

She is always saying no. I think it is ill-natured of her.

JACK: Oh, Gwendolen is fine. As far as she is concerned, we are engaged. Her mother is perfectly awful. She is a monster. I beg your pardon, Algy. I shouldn't talk about your own aunt like that to you.

ALGERNON: My dear boy, I love hearing my relatives abused. It is the only thing that makes me put up with them at all. Relatives are dull people. They don't know how to live or when to die.

JACK: Oh, that is nonsense!

ALGERNON: It isn't!

JACK: I won't argue. You always want to argue about things.

ALGERNON: That is exactly what things are for.

JACK: If I thought that, I'd give up. (*a pause*) You don't think there is any chance Gwendolen will become like her mother, do you, Algy?

ALGERNON: All women become like their mothers. That is their tragedy. No man does. That's his.

JACK: Is that supposed to be clever?

ALGERNON: It sounds good! It is as true as any remark in civilized life should be.

JACK: I am sick to death of cleverness. Everybody is clever. You can't go anywhere without meeting clever people. I wish we had a few fools left.

ALGERNON: We have.

JACK: I should like to meet them. What do they talk about?

ALGERNON: The fools? Oh, about the clever people, of course.

JACK: What fools!

ALGERNON: By the way, did you tell Gwendolen you are Ernest in town and Jack in the country?

JACK (*in a very lordly way*): My dear fellow, one does not tell the truth to a nice, sweet girl. What odd ideas you have about how to act toward a woman!

ALGERNON: The only way to act toward a woman is to flirt with her if she is pretty and with someone else if she is plain.

JACK: Oh, that is nonsense.

ALGERNON: What about your brother? What about the wicked Ernest?

JACK: Oh, soon I will get rid of him. I'll say he died in Paris of a stroke. Lots of people die of a stroke quickly, don't they?

ALGERNON: Yes, but it runs in families. You should say he had a severe chill.

JACK: You are sure a severe chill doesn't run in families?

ALGERNON: Of course it doesn't!

JACK: Very well, then. My poor brother Ernest dies suddenly in Paris, from a severe chill. That gets rid of him.

ALGERNON: I thought you said that Miss Cardew was too interested in your poor brother Ernest. Won't she feel his loss?

JACK: No. Cecily is not a silly girl. She eats well, goes for long walks, and pays no attention at all to her lessons.

ALGERNON: I would like to meet Cecily.

JACK: I shall make sure you never do. She is very pretty, and she is only 18.

ALGERNON: Have you told Gwendolen yet that you have a very pretty, eighteen-year-old girl under your care?

JACK: Oh, one doesn't just tell these things to people. Cecily and Gwendolen are sure to be great friends. I'll bet you anything that half an hour after they have met, they will be calling each other sister.

ALGERNON: Women only do that when they have called each other many other things first. Now, if we want to get a good table at the restaurant, we really must dress. It is nearly seven.

JACK: Oh, it is always nearly seven.

ALGERNON: Well, I'm hungry.

JACK: You are always hungry.

ALGERNON: What shall we do after dinner? Go to
   a theater?

JACK: Oh, no! I hate listening.

ALGERNON: Shall we go to the Club?

JACK: Oh, no! I hate talking.

ALGERNON: Well, what shall we do?

JACK: Nothing!

ALGERNON: It is awfully hard work doing nothing.

(LANE *enters.*)

LANE (*announcing a visitor*): Miss Fairfax.

(GWENDOLEN *enters.* LANE *goes out.*)

ALGERNON: Gwendolen!

GWENDOLEN: Algy, kindly turn your back. I have
   something to say to Mr. Worthing.

(ALGERNON *goes to the fireplace.*)

JACK: My own darling!

GWENDOLEN: Ernest, we may never be married.
   From the expression on Mamma's face,
   it seems unlikely. Few parents today care
   what their children say. The old-fashioned
   respect for the young is dying out.
   Whatever control I had over Mamma, I lost
   at the age of three. She may not let us
   become man and wife. I may marry
   someone else. I may marry often. Yet,
   nothing can change my love for you.

JACK: Dear Gwendolen.

GWENDOLEN: The romantic story of your origin in the railway station has stirred my deepest nature. Your first name has a strong interest. Your simplicity makes you mysterious. Your town address I have. What is your address in the country?

JACK: The Manor House, Woolton, Hertfordshire. (ALGERNON, *who has been listening, smiles to himself. He writes the address on his shirt cuff. He then picks up the railway schedule.*)

GWENDOLEN: The postal service is good, I hope? I may need to do something desperate. That will require deep thought. I will write daily.

JACK: My own one!

GWENDOLEN: How much longer are you in town?

JACK: Till Monday.

GWENDOLEN: Good! Algy, you may turn around.

ALGERNON: Thanks, I've turned around already.

GWENDOLEN: You may also ring the bell. (ALGERNON *obeys.*)

JACK: May I see you to your carriage, darling?

GWENDOLEN: Certainly.

JACK (*to* LANE, *who now enters*): I will see Miss Fairfax out.

LANE: Yes, sir. (JACK *and* GWENDOLEN *go off.* LANE *presents several letters on a platter to* ALGERNON. *They are bills.* ALGERNON, *after looking at the envelopes, tears them up.*)

ALGERNON: A glass of sherry, Lane.

LANE: Yes, sir.

ALGERNON: Tomorrow, Lane, I'm going Bunburying.

LANE: Yes, sir.

ALGERNON: I shall not be back till Monday. You can pack my dress clothes. Also, please pack all the Bunbury suits.

LANE: Yes, sir. (*handing the sherry*)

ALGERNON: I hope tomorrow will be fine, Lane.

LANE: It never is, sir.

ALGERNON: Lane, you are so gloomy.

LANE: I do my best to please, sir.

(JACK *enters.* LANE *goes off.*)

JACK: There's a sensible, smart girl! The only girl I ever cared for. (ALGERNON *is laughing.*) What are you so amused at?

ALGERNON: Oh, I'm worried about poor Bunbury.

JACK: If you don't take care, your friend Bunbury will get you into a serious problem.

ALGERNON: I love problems. They are the only things that are never serious.

JACK: Oh that's nonsense, Algy. You only speak nonsense.

ALGERNON: Everyone does.

(JACK *looks angrily at him. He leaves the room.* ALGERNON *reads his shirt cuff and smiles.*)

Curtain

Act 2

The garden at the Manor House. Gray stone steps lead to the house. The garden is full of roses. It is July. Chairs and a table covered with books are set under a large tree. Miss Prism is seated at the table. Cecily is in the back, watering flowers.

Miss Prism (*calling*): Cecily, Cecily! Watering the flowers is a servant's job, not yours. At this moment, your schooling awaits. Your German grammar is on the table. Please open it at page 15. We will repeat yesterday's lesson.

Cecily (*coming over very slowly*): I don't like German. It isn't a language that makes me look good. I know that I look quite plain after my German lesson.

Miss Prism: Child, you know how much your guardian wants you to improve yourself. He mentioned your German as he was leaving for town yesterday. Indeed, he always mentions your German when he is leaving.

Cecily: Dear Uncle Jack is so serious! Sometimes he is so serious I think he cannot be quite well.

Miss Prism (*drawing herself up*): Your guardian enjoys the best of health. His serious manner is to be praised in one so young. I know no one who has a higher sense of duty.

CECILY: I guess that is why he often looks a little bored when we three are together.

MISS PRISM: Cecily! I am surprised at you. Mr. Worthing has many troubles in his life. Fun would be out of place in his talk. You must remember he worries about that sad young man, his brother.

CECILY: I wish Uncle Jack would allow that sad young man, his brother, to visit. We might have a good influence on him, Miss Prism. I am sure you would. You know German and geology. Things like that influence a man very much. (*She begins to write in her diary.*)

MISS PRISM (*shaking her head*): I do not think that even I could help someone who is so weak. I am not sure that I would want to save him. I do not like this modern way of turning bad people into good people at a moment's notice. You must put away your diary, Cecily. I don't see why you keep a diary at all.

CECILY: I keep a diary to write the wonderful secrets of my life. If I didn't write them, I would probably forget all about them.

MISS PRISM: Memory, dear Cecily, is the diary that we all carry with us.

CECILY: Yes, but it often records things that have not happened. I think Memory is to blame for nearly all the longer novels I get from the library.

MISS PRISM: Do not speak ill of the longer novel, Cecily. I wrote one myself in earlier days.

CECILY: Did you really, Miss Prism? How clever you are! I hope it did not end happily. I don't like novels that end happily. They depress me.

MISS PRISM: The good ended happily. The bad ended unhappily. That is what Fiction is.

CECILY: I suppose so. Yet, it seems very unfair. Was your novel ever published?

MISS PRISM: Alas! No. The text was lost. To your work, child. This talk is useless.

CECILY (*smiling*): I see Dr. Chasuble coming.

MISS PRISM (*rising*): Dr. Chasuble! This is a pleasure.

(CANON CHASUBLE *enters, wearing the clothing of a country minister.*)

CANON CHASUBLE: How are we this morning? Miss Prism, you are, I hope, well?

CECILY: Miss Prism has just been saying she had a slight headache. It would do her so much good to have a stroll with you in the park, Dr. Chasuble.

MISS PRISM (*scolding*): Cecily, I have not said anything about a headache.

CECILY: No, dear Miss Prism, I know that. I felt, though, that you had a headache. I was thinking about that, and not about my German lesson, when the minister came in.

CANON CHASUBLE: I hope, Cecily, you are studying hard.

CECILY: Oh, I am afraid I am.

CANON CHASUBLE: Mr. Worthing has not returned from town yet?

MISS PRISM: We do not expect him till Monday.

CANON CHASUBLE: Ah, yes, he does like to spend his Sundays in London. He is not one of those whose only aim is enjoyment. By all accounts, that is the aim of that sad young man, his brother. Now, you will want to get back to your work. I shall see you both at evening service.

MISS PRISM: I think, dear Doctor, I will have a stroll. I do have a headache after all. A walk might help.

CANON CHASUBLE: With pleasure, Miss Prism. We might go as far as the school and back.

MISS PRISM: That would be delightful. Cecily, you will read your Political Economy. (*She goes through the garden with* DR. CHASUBLE.)

CECILY (*picking up the books and throwing them back on the table*): Horrid Political Economy! Horrid Geography! Horrid, horrid German!

(MERRIMAN *enters with a card on a silver platter.*)

MERRIMAN: Mr. Ernest Worthing has just driven over from the station with his luggage.

CECILY (*taking the card and reading it*): "Mr. Ernest Worthing, B4, The Albany."

Uncle Jack's brother! Did you tell him Mr. Worthing was in London?

MERRIMAN: Yes, Miss. He seemed very sad. I told him you and Miss Prism were in the garden. He said he wanted to speak to you alone.

CECILY: Ask Mr. Ernest Worthing to come here. Please ask the housekeeper about a room for him.

MERRIMAN: Yes, Miss. (*He goes out.*)

CECILY: I have never met any really wicked person before. I am frightened. I am so afraid he will look just like everyone else.

(ALGERNON *enters, charming and elegant.*)

CECILY: He does!

ALGERNON (*raising his hat*): You are my little Cousin Cecily, I'm sure.

CECILY (*looking at him slowly*): You have made a mistake. I am not little. I am tall for my age. (ALGERNON *is rather taken aback.*) Still, I am your Cousin Cecily. You, I see from your card, are Uncle Jack's brother. You are my wicked Cousin Ernest.

ALGERNON: Oh! I am not wicked at all, Cousin Cecily. Please don't think I am wicked.

CECILY: If you are not, then you have been lying to us all. I hope you have not been leading a double life. Have you been acting as if you were wicked while really being good all this time? That would not be right.

ALGERNON (*looking at her in amazement*): Oh! Well, I have been rather wild.

CECILY: I am glad to hear it.

ALGERNON (*suddenly seeing how he can win* CECILY'S *favor*): In fact, I have been very bad in my own small way.

CECILY: You should not be proud of that. I am sure it must have been pleasant, though.

ALGERNON: It is more pleasant being with you.

CECILY: I can't understand how you are here at all. Uncle Jack won't be back till Monday afternoon.

ALGERNON: That saddens me greatly. I must go back to London on Monday.

CECILY: You should wait until Uncle Jack arrives. He wants to talk to you about your leaving.

ALGERNON: About my what?

CECILY: Your leaving. He has gone to buy your outfit.

ALGERNON: I wouldn't let Jack buy my outfit. He has no taste in neckties at all.

CECILY: I don't think you will need neckties. Uncle Jack is sending you to Australia.

ALGERNON (*with great disgust*): Australia! I'd sooner die!

CECILY: Well, he said at dinner on Wednesday night that you could choose between this world, the next, and Australia.

ALGERNON: Oh, well! What I have heard of Australia and the next world do not sound good. This world is fine for me, Cousin Cecily.

CECILY: Yes, but are you fine for it?

ALGERNON (*sighing*): I'm afraid I'm not. (*very seriously*) That is why I want you to make me a better person. You could make that your job, Cousin Cecily.

CECILY: I'm afraid I don't have time this afternoon.

ALGERNON: Well, would you mind if I became a better person by myself this afternoon?

CECILY: That is rather unlikely. You can try if you want to.

ALGERNON: I will. I feel better already.

CECILY: You are looking a little worse.

ALGERNON: That is because I am hungry.

CECILY: How selfish of me. I should have remembered that when one is going to lead a new life, one needs regular meals. Please come in.

ALGERNON: Thank you. May I have a flower to put on my coat first? I never feel like eating unless I have a flower on my coat.

CECILY: A yellow rose? (*picks up scissors*)

ALGERNON: No, I'd like a pink rose.

CECILY: Why? (*cuts a flower*)

ALGERNON: Because you are like a pink rose, Cousin Cecily.

CECILY: I don't think it is right for you to talk to me like that. Miss Prism never talks like that to me.

ALGERNON: Then, Miss Prism is an unthinking old lady. (CECILY *puts the rose in the buttonhole of his lapel.*) You are the prettiest girl I ever saw.

CECILY (*matter-of-factly*): Miss Prism says that good looks are a trap.

ALGERNON: They are a trap any sensible man would like to be caught in.

CECILY (*lightly*): Oh! I don't want to catch a sensible man. I wouldn't know what to talk to him about.

(*They walk into the house.* MISS PRISM *and* CANON CHASUBLE *return.*)

MISS PRISM (*tenderly*): You are too much alone, dear Dr. Chasuble. You should get married.

CANON CHASUBLE (*with a shudder*): The Ancient Church was quite against marriage.

MISS PRISM (*pointedly*): That is surely why the Ancient Church has not lasted up to now. You do not seem to realize, dear Doctor, that by staying single, a man becomes a temptation. Men should be careful. This belief against marriage leads some weaker women astray.

CANON CHASUBLE (*in wonder*): Is a man not as attractive when married?

MISS PRISM: A married man is only attractive to his wife.

CANON CHASUBLE: Often, I've been told, not even to her.

MISS PRISM: That depends on the intelligence of the woman. Maturity in a woman means she can be counted on. (CANON CHASUBLE *looks startled.*) Where is Cecily?

CANON CHASUBLE: Perhaps she followed us.

(JACK *enters slowly from the back of the garden. He is dressed in black, as if someone has died.*)

MISS PRISM (*startled*): Mr. Worthing!

CANON CHASUBLE (*gently asking*): Mr. Worthing?

MISS PRISM: This is a surprise. We did not expect you till Monday afternoon.

JACK (*shaking hands in a tragic way*): I have come back sooner than I expected. Dr. Chasuble, I hope you are well?

CANON CHASUBLE: Dear Mr. Worthing, I trust these clothes do not mean a terrible tragedy has happened?

JACK: My brother.

MISS PRISM: More debts and careless spending?

CANON CHASUBLE: Still leading his life of pleasure?

JACK (*very dramatically*): Dead!

CANON CHASUBLE: Your brother Ernest is dead?

JACK: Quite dead.

MISS PRISM (*as if satisfied*): What a lesson for him! I hope he will learn from it.

CANON CHASUBLE: Mr. Worthing, I offer you my sympathy. You at least know you were the most generous and forgiving of brothers.

JACK (*with a great sigh*): Poor Ernest! He had many faults. Even so, it is a sad, sad blow.

CANON CHASUBLE: Very sad. Were you with him at the end?

JACK: No, he died in Paris. I had a telegram from the manager of his hotel there.

CANON CHASUBLE: Did it give the cause of death?

JACK: A severe chill, it seems.

MISS PRISM: A man shall pay for the life he lived.

CANON CHASUBLE (*raising his hand*): Charity, dear Miss Prism! None of us are perfect. I myself easily catch chills. Will he be buried here?

JACK: No. He wanted to be buried in Paris.

CANON CHASUBLE: In Paris! (*shaking his head*) I fear that hardly points to a serious state of mind at the end of his life. You will, of course, wish me to make some small mention of your tragic loss next Sunday. (JACK *presses his hand.*) I have a sermon that can be used for almost any event. It can be joyful or, as in this case, sad. (*All sigh.*) I have preached it at celebrations and christenings.

JACK: Ah, that reminds me. You said
christenings, I think, Dr. Chasuble.
I suppose you know how to christen?
(CANON CHASUBLE *looks amazed.*) I mean,
you are always christening, aren't you?

MISS PRISM: It is, I am sad to say, one of the
minister's more constant duties.

CANON CHASUBLE (*approaching the subject
delicately*): Is there a baby who needs
to be christened, Mr. Worthing? Your
brother was not married, was he?

JACK: Oh, no.

MISS PRISM (*bitterly*): People who live just
for pleasure rarely are.

JACK: It is not for a child, Doctor. The fact is,
I would like to be christened myself. This
afternoon, if you have nothing better to do.

CANON CHASUBLE: But surely, Mr. Worthing, you
have been christened already?

JACK: I don't remember anything about it.
Of course, I don't know if you think I am
a little too old now.

CANON CHASUBLE: Not at all. The sprinkling, and
indeed, the dipping under water of adults
is often done.

JACK: Under water!

CANON CHASUBLE: Have no fears. Sprinkling is all
that is needed or even sensible. Our weather
is so changeable. When do you wish to have
the ceremony?

JACK: Oh, I might come by around 5:00 P.M. if that would suit you.

CANON CHASUBLE: Perfectly, perfectly! In fact, I have two others at that time. A case of twins born in one of the cottages on your own estate. Poor Jenkins, a most hard working man.

JACK: Oh! I don't see much fun in being christened along with babies. It would be childish. Would half-past five do?

CANON CHASUBLE: That would be fine. (*He takes out his watch.*) Now, dear Mr. Worthing, I will not intrude any longer in a house of sorrow. I would just beg you not to be too weighed down by grief. What seem to us tragic events may be blessings in disguise.

MISS PRISM: This seems to me a blessing not in disguise.

(CECILY *enters from the house.*)

CECILY: Uncle Jack! Oh, I am so pleased to see you back. What horrid clothes you have on! Do go and change them.

MISS PRISM (*sternly*): Cecily!

CANON CHASUBLE (*gently*): My child! My child! (CECILY *goes toward* JACK. *He sadly kisses her forehead.*)

CECILY: What is wrong, Uncle Jack? Do look happy! You look as if you had a toothache,

and I have such a surprise for you.
Who do you think is in the dining room?
Your brother!

JACK (*blankly*): Who?

CECILY (*with excitement*): Your brother Ernest.
He arrived about half an hour ago.

JACK (*annoyed and confused*): What nonsense!
I don't have a brother.

Cecily (*sweetly*): Oh, don't say that. However
badly he may have behaved to you in the
past, he is still your brother. I'll tell him to
come out. You will shake hands with him,
won't you, Uncle Jack? (*She runs back into
the house.*)

CANON CHASUBLE (*full of doubt, but saying the
correct thing anyway*): This is very
joyful news.

MISS PRISM (*bluntly*): After we had all been used
to his loss, his sudden return is odd.

JACK (*in a daze*): My brother is in the dining
room? I don't know what it all means. I think
it is perfectly silly.

(ALGERNON *and* CECILY *enter hand in hand. They
come slowly up to* JACK.)

JACK: Good heavens! (*waves* ALGERNON *away*)

ALGERNON: Brother Jack, I am very sorry for all
the trouble I have given you. I plan to lead
a better life in the future. (JACK *glares at
him. He will not take his hand.*)

CECILY: Uncle Jack, you are not going to take your brother's hand?

JACK: Nothing will persuade me to take his hand. I think his being here is shameful. He knows very well why.

CECILY: Uncle Jack, do be nice. There is some good in everyone. Ernest has just been telling me about his poor ill friend, Mr. Bunbury. He goes to visit him so often. There must be good in one who is kind to a sick person and leaves the pleasures of London to sit by his bed.

JACK: Oh, he has been talking about Bunbury, has he?

CECILY: Yes, he has told me all about poor Mr. Bunbury and his bad health.

JACK (*angrily*): Bunbury! I won't have him talk to you about Bunbury or about anything else. It is enough to drive one crazy.

ALGERNON: Of course, I know of the bad things I have done. I still think Brother Jack's coldness to me is painful. I expected a happier welcome. After all, it is the first time I have come here.

CECILY: Uncle Jack, if you don't shake hands with Ernest, I will never forgive you.

JACK (*taken aback*): Never forgive me?

CECILY (*in a childish tone*): Never, never, never!

JACK: Well, this is the last time I shall ever do it. (*He shakes hands with* ALGERNON *and glares.*)

CANON CHASUBLE: It's lovely, is it not, to see so perfect a reunion? I think we should leave the two brothers together.

MISS PRISM: Cecily, you will come with us.

CECILY (*satisfied*): Of course, Miss Prism. My task is done.

CANON CHASUBLE: You have done a beautiful thing today, dear child.

MISS PRISM: We must not be quick in our judgments.

CECILY: I feel very happy. (*They all go off.*)

JACK: You young rascal, Algy. You must get out of here as soon as possible. I don't allow any Bunburying here.

(MERRIMAN *enters.*)

MERRIMAN: I have put Mr. Ernest's things in the room next to yours, sir. Is that all right?

JACK: What?

MERRIMAN: Mr. Ernest's luggage, sir. I have unpacked it and put it in the room next to your own.

JACK: His luggage?

MERRIMAN: Yes, sir. Three large suitcases, a smaller one, two hatboxes, and a large lunch basket.

ALGERNON: I'm afraid I can't stay more than a week this time.

JACK: Merriman, order the carriage at once. Mr. Ernest has been called back to town.

MERRIMAN: Yes, sir. (*He goes back into the house.*)

ALGERNON: What a fearful liar you are, Jack. I have not been called back to town at all.

JACK (*coldly*): Yes, you have.

ALGERNON: I haven't heard anyone call me.

JACK: Your duty as a gentleman calls you back.

ALGERNON (*smiling wickedly*): My duty as a gentleman never gets in the way of my pleasures.

JACK: I can see that.

ALGERNON: Well, Cecily is a darling.

JACK: You are not to talk of Miss Cardew like that. I don't like it.

ALGERNON: Well, I don't like your clothes. You look perfectly silly in them. Why don't you go up and change? It is childish to be in deep sorrow for a man who is staying here as your guest for the week.

JACK: You are not staying with me for a week as a guest or anything else. You have to leave on the 4:00 P.M. train.

ALGERNON: I won't leave you when you are so sad. It would be most unfriendly. If I were in sorrow, you would stay with me, I think. I would think it very unkind if you didn't.

JACK: Well, will you go if I change my clothes?

ALGERNON: Yes, if you are not too long. I never saw anybody take so long to dress. The time you spend doesn't seem to make much difference anyway.

JACK: Well, at any rate, that is better than always being overdressed as you are.

ALGERNON: If I am sometimes a little overdressed, I make up for it by being so very overeducated.

JACK: You are overly proud of yourself. Your conduct is an outrage. Your being in my garden is absurd. However, you have to catch the 4:00 P.M. train. I hope you will have a nice journey back to town. This Bunburying, as you call it, has not been a great success for you. (*He goes into the house.*)

ALGERNON: I think it has been a great success. I'm in love with Cecily. That is everything. (CECILY *enters at the back of the garden. She picks up the watering can and begins to water the flowers.*) I must see her before I go and make plans for another Bunbury. Ah, there she is.

CECILY: I just came back to water the roses. I thought you were with Uncle Jack.

ALGERNON: He's gone to order the carriage for me.

CECILY: Oh, is he going to take you for a nice drive?

ALGERNON: He's going to send me away.

CECILY (*pouting*): Then, we must part?

ALGERNON: I am afraid so. It's very painful.

CECILY (*as if repeating from memory*): It is always painful to part from people one has known only a short time. When old friends leave, the parting is easy to deal with. Parting from a person one has just met is awful.

ALGERNON: Thank you.

(MERRIMAN *enters.*)

MERRIMAN: The carriage is at the door, sir. (ALGERNON *looks hopefully at* CECILY.)

CECILY: It can wait, Merriman . . . for . . . five minutes.

MERRIMAN: Yes, miss. (*He leaves.*)

ALGERNON: I hope, Cecily, I shall not anger you if I tell you something openly. I think you are in every way perfect.

CECILY: I think your openness does you great credit, Ernest. If you will let me, I will copy your remarks into my diary. (*She goes over to the table and begins writing in her diary.*)

ALGERNON: Do you really keep a diary? I'd give anything to look at it. May I?

CECILY: Oh, no. (*putting her hand over it*) You see, it is simply a young girl's record of her own thoughts and feelings. Because of that, it is meant to be published. When it is, I hope you will buy a copy. Please, Ernest, don't stop. I delight in writing what people say. I have reached the part where you said I am "in every way perfect." You can go on. I am ready for more.

ALGERNON (*somewhat taken aback*): Ahem! Ahem!

CECILY (*mocking the stiff manner of* MISS PRISM): Oh, don't cough, Ernest. When one is speaking words to be copied, one should speak smoothly. Besides, I don't know how to spell a cough. (*She writes as* ALGERNON *speaks.*)

ALGERNON (*talking very rapidly*): Cecily, ever since I first looked upon your beauty, I have dared to love you wildly, hopelessly, completely.

CECILY: I don't think you should tell me that you love me wildly, hopelessly, completely. Hopelessly doesn't make much sense, does it?

ALGERNON (*joyfully*): Cecily!

(MERRIMAN *enters.*)

MERRIMAN: The carriage is waiting, sir.

ALGERNON: Tell it to come around next week, at the same hour.

MERRIMAN (*looks at* CECILY, *who gives no sign*): Yes, sir. (*He leaves.*)

CECILY: Uncle Jack would be very upset if he knew you were staying on till next week, at the same hour.

ALGERNON: Oh, I don't care about Jack. I don't care for anybody in the whole world but you. I love you, Cecily. (*taking her hands*) You will marry me, won't you?

CECILY: You silly you! Of course. Why, we have been engaged for the last three months.

ALGERNON: (*letting go of her hands in wonder*): For the last three months?

CECILY: Yes, it will be three months on Thursday.

ALGERNON: How did we become engaged?

CECILY: Well, dear Uncle Jack told us he had a younger brother who was very wicked. Since then, you have been the only thing Miss Prism and I have talked about. A man who is much talked about is always very attractive. One feels there must be something in him after all. I know it was foolish of me, but I fell in love with you, Ernest.

ALGERNON: Darling! When was the engagement actually settled?

CECILY: On the fourth of February. You did not seem to know that I existed, so I decided to end the matter. After a long struggle with myself, I said I would marry you. The next day, I bought this little bracelet with the true lover's knot I promised always to wear.

ALGERNON (*looking at the bracelet*): Did I give you this? It's very pretty, isn't it?

CECILY: Yes. You have very good taste, Ernest. It's the excuse I've always given for your leading such a bad life. Here is the box in which I keep all your dear letters. (*She kneels at the table and opens the box. Then, she shows him the letters tied up with blue ribbon.*)

ALGERNON: My letters! But my own sweet Cecily, I have never written you any letters.

CECILY (*gently scolding*): I know that, Ernest. I remember only too well that I had to write your letters for you. I wrote three times a week. Sometimes more often.

ALGERNON: Oh, may I read them, Cecily?

CECILY: Oh, I couldn't. They would make you far too pleased with yourself. (*She puts back the box.*) The three you wrote to me after I broke off the engagement are so beautiful and so badly spelled. Even now, I can hardly read them without crying a little.

ALGERNON: Was our engagement broken off?

CECILY: Of course, it was. On the 22nd of March. You can see the entry if you like. (*shows him the diary*) "Today I broke off my engagement with Ernest. I feel it is better to do so. The weather continues to be charming."

ALGERNON: Why did you break it off? What had I done? I had done nothing at all. Cecily, I am very much hurt to hear you broke it off—even when the weather was so charming.

CECILY: It would hardly have been a really serious engagement if it hadn't been broken off at least once. I forgave you before the week was out.

ALGERNON (*crossing to her and kneeling*): What a perfect angel you are, Cecily.

CECILY: You dear romantic boy. (*He kisses her. She puts her fingers through his hair.*) I hope your hair curls naturally. Does it?

ALGERNON: Yes darling, with a little help from others.

CECILY: I'm so glad.

ALGERNON: You'll never break off our engagement again, Cecily?

CECILY: I don't think I could break it off now that I have really met you. Besides, of course, there is the question of your name.

ALGERNON (*nervously*): Yes, of course.

CECILY: You must not laugh at me, darling. It had always been a girlish dream of mine to love someone named Ernest. (ALGERNON *rises;* CECILY *also.*) There is something in that name that inspires total faith. I pity any woman whose husband is not called Ernest.

ALGERNON: My dear child, do you mean to say you could not love me if I had some other name?

CECILY: What other name?

ALGERNON (*forcing himself to sound casual*): Oh, any name you like—Algernon, for example.

CECILY: I don't like the name of Algernon.

ALGERNON: Well, my own dear, sweet, loving little darling, I don't know why you object to the name of Algernon. It is not at all a bad name. In fact, it is a rather noble name. Cecily, (*moving to her*) if my name were Algy, could you love me?

CECILY (*rising*): I might respect you, Ernest. I might admire you. However, I fear that I should not be able to give you my full attention if your name were not Ernest.

ALGERNON: Ahem! Cecily! (*picking up his hat*) Your minister here knows all the ceremonies of the Church?

CECILY: Oh, yes. Dr. Chasuble is a most learned man. He has never written a single book. You can imagine how much he knows.

ALGERNON: I must see him at once on a most important christening—I mean on most important business.

CECILY: Oh!

ALGERNON: I should not be away more than half an hour.

CECILY (*looking hurt*): We have been engaged since February 14th. I only met you today for the first time. I think it is too bad that you should leave me for so long as half an hour. Couldn't you make it 20 minutes?

ALGERNON: I'll be back in no time. (*He kisses her and rushes through the garden.*)

CECILY: He is so full of surprises. I like his hair so much. I must enter his proposal in my diary.

(MERRIMAN *enters.*)

MERRIMAN: A Miss Fairfax has just called to see Mr. Worthing. On very important business, Miss Fairfax states.

CECILY: Isn't Mr. Worthing in his library?

MERRIMAN: Mr. Worthing went over toward the church some time ago.

CECILY: Please ask the lady to come out here. Mr. Worthing is sure to be back soon. You can bring tea.

MERRIMAN: Yes, Miss. (*He goes out.*)

CECILY (*thinking aloud*): Miss Fairfax! I guess this must be one of the many older women who help Uncle Jack in his charity work in London. I don't quite like women who are interested in charity. I think it is so bold of them.

(MERRIMAN *enters.*)

MERRIMAN: Miss Fairfax.

(GWENDOLEN *enters.* MERRIMAN *exits.*)

CECILY (*meeting her*): Please let me introduce myself. My name is Cecily Cardew.

GWENDOLEN: Cecily Cardew? (*moving to her and shaking hands*) What a very sweet name!

Something tells me that we are going to be great friends. I like you already more than I can say. My first feelings about people are never wrong.

CECILY: How nice of you to like me so much after we have known each other such a short time. Please sit down.

GWENDOLEN (*still standing up*): May I call you Cecily?

CECILY: With pleasure!

GWENDOLEN: You will always call me Gwendolen, won't you?

CECILY: If you wish.

GWENDOLEN: Then, that is all settled, is it not?

CECILY: I hope so. (*A pause. They sit down together.*)

GWENDOLEN (*with an air of being better than* CECILY): This might be a good time for me to say who I am. My father is Lord Bracknell. You have never heard of Papa, I suppose?

CECILY: I don't think so.

GWENDOLEN: Outside the family, I am glad to say, no one knows Papa. I think that is quite as it should be. The home seems to me the proper place for the man. Mamma, whose views on education are very strict, has brought me up to be very limited in my thinking. It is part of her system. Do you mind my looking at you through my glasses?

CECILY: Oh, not at all, Gwendolen. I am very fond of being looked at.

GWENDOLEN (*after looking at* CECILY *carefully through her glasses*): You are here on a short visit, I suppose.

CECILY: Oh no! I live here.

GWENDOLEN (*severely*): Really? Your mother, no doubt, or some older female relative, lives here also?

CECILY: Oh no! I have no mother, nor, in fact, any family.

GWENDOLEN: Indeed?

CECILY: My dear guardian, with the help of Miss Prism, has the difficult task of looking after me.

GWENDOLEN: Your guardian?

CECILY: Yes, I am Mr. Worthing's ward.

GWENDOLEN (*raising her eyebrows*): Oh! It is strange. He never said he had a ward. How secretive of him! He grows more interesting hourly. I am not sure, however, that the news leaves me feeling happy. (*rising and going to her*) I am very fond of you, Cecily. I have liked you ever since I met you. I must say that now that I know that you are Mr. Worthing's ward, I cannot help wishing you were a little older and not quite so pretty. If I may speak openly—

CECILY: Please do! I think that whenever one has anything unpleasant to say, one should be quite open.

GWENDOLEN: Well, to speak with perfect openness, Cecily, I wish that you were 42 and plain for your age. Ernest has a strong, honest nature. He is the very soul of truth and honor. Falseness would be as unlikely for him as lying. However, even men of noble character are at risk to the beauty of others. Modern as well as ancient history gives us many painful examples of this. If it were not so, history would be quite unreadable.

CECILY: I beg your pardon, Gwendolen. Did you say Ernest?

GWENDOLEN: Yes.

CECILY: Oh, but it is not Mr. Ernest Worthing who is my guardian. It is his brother—his elder brother.

GWENDOLEN (*sitting down again*): Ernest never told me he had a brother.

CECILY: I am sorry to say they have not been on good terms for a long time.

GWENDOLEN: Ah! That explains it. Now that I think of it, I have never heard any man talk about his brother. The subject seems distasteful to most men. Cecily, you have lifted a load from my mind. I was growing almost worried. It would have been terrible if any cloud had come across a friendship like ours. You are quite sure that Mr. Ernest Worthing is not your guardian?

CECILY: Quite sure. (*a pause*) In fact, I am going to be his.

GWENDOLEN (*questioningly*): I beg your pardon?

CECILY (*rather shyly*): Dearest Gwendolen, there is no reason why I should not tell you. Our little county newspaper is sure to report the fact next week. Mr. Ernest Worthing and I are to be married.

GWENDOLEN (*quite politely, rising*): My darling Cecily, I think there must be some slight error. Mr. Ernest Worthing is engaged to me. The announcement will appear in the *Morning Post* on Saturday.

CECILY (*very politely, rising*): I am afraid you are wrong. Ernest asked me to marry him exactly ten minutes ago. (*shows her diary*)

GWENDOLEN (*looking at the diary through her glasses*): It is very curious. He asked me to be his wife yesterday afternoon at 5:30 P.M. If you would care to see the proof, please do so. (*shows diary of her own*) I never travel without my diary. One should always have something thrilling to read on the train. I am so sorry, dear Cecily, if it is a disappointment to you, but I am afraid I have the first claim. He asked me first.

CECILY: It would upset me more than I can tell you, dear Gwendolen, if I cause you any pain. However, I must point out that in the time since Ernest asked you to marry him, he clearly has changed his mind.

GWENDOLEN (*thoughtfully*): Perhaps the poor fellow has been trapped into a foolish promise. I shall rescue him at once—and with a firm hand.

CECILY (*thoughtfully and sadly*): Whatever mess my dear boy may have gotten into, I will never scold him about it after we are married.

GWENDOLEN: Do you refer to me, Miss Cardew, as a mess? At a time like this, it becomes more than a duty to speak one's mind. It becomes a pleasure.

CECILY (*with rising anger*): Do you suggest, Miss Fairfax, that I trapped Ernest into an engagement? How dare you? This is no time for being polite.

GWENDOLEN: It is clear that our social worlds have been very different.

(MERRIMAN *enters, followed by another male servant who assists him. He carries a platter, tablecloth, and plate stand.* CECILY *is about to speak. The presence of the servants, however, stops the discussion. Both girls suffer from not being able to express themselves.*)

MERRIMAN: Shall I set tea here as usual, Miss?

CECILY (*sternly, in a calm voice*): Yes, as usual. (MERRIMAN *begins to clear the table and place the cloth. A long pause.* CECILY *and* GWENDOLEN *glare at each other.*)

GWENDOLEN: Are there many interesting walks near here, Miss Cardew?

CECILY: Oh! Yes! A great many. From the top of one of the close by hills, one can see five counties.

GWENDOLEN: Five counties! I don't think I should like that. I hate crowds.

CECILY (*sweetly*): I suppose that is why you live in town? (GWENDOLEN *bites her lip. She beats her foot nervously with her umbrella.*)

GWENDOLEN (*looking around*): Quite a well-kept garden this is, Miss Cardew.

CECILY: So glad you like it, Miss Fairfax.

GWENDOLEN: I had no idea there were any flowers in the country.

CECILY: Oh, flowers are as common here, Miss Fairfax, as people are in London.

GWENDOLEN: I cannot understand how anybody manages to live in the country, if anybody who is anybody does. The country always bores me to death.

CECILY: Ah! I believe the nobility are suffering very much from boredom right now. It is a real problem with them, I have been told. May I offer you some tea, Miss Fairfax?

GWENDOLEN (*with studied politeness*): Thank you. (*aside*) Hateful girl! I need tea, but I hate to take it from her.

CECILY (*sweetly*): Sugar?

GWENDOLEN (*scornfully*): No, thank you. No one uses sugar any more. (CECILY *looks angrily at her. She takes the tongs and puts four lumps of sugar into* GWENDOLEN'S *cup.*)

CECILY (*severely*): Cake or bread and butter?

GWENDOLEN (*in a bored manner*): Bread and butter, please. Cake is rarely seen at the best houses these days.

CECILY (*cuts a very large slice of cake and puts it on the tray*): Hand that to Miss Fairfax. (MERRIMAN *does so. He then goes out with the other servant.* GWENDOLEN *drinks the tea and shudders. Puts down cup at once. She reaches her hand to the bread and butter, looks at it, and finds it is cake. She rises in anger.*)

GWENDOLEN: You have filled my tea with lumps of sugar. Though I asked for bread and butter, you have given me cake. I am known for my gentleness and sweetness. I warn you, Miss Cardew, you may go too far.

CECILY (*rising*): I would do anything to save my poor, innocent, trusting boy from the tricks of any other girl.

GWENDOLEN: From the moment I saw you, I did not trust you. I felt that you were false and lying. I am never wrong in such matters. My first feelings about people are always right.

CECILY: It seems to me, Miss Fairfax, that I am taking up your time. No doubt you have many similar calls to make in the neighborhood.

(JACK *enters.*)

GWENDOLEN (*seeing him*): Ernest! My own Ernest!

JACK: Gwendolen! Darling! (*offers to kiss her*)

GWENDOLEN (*moving back*): A moment! May I ask if you are engaged to be married to this young lady? (*pointing to* CECILY)

JACK (*laughing*): To dear little Cecily! Of course not! What could have put such an idea into your pretty little head?

GWENDOLEN: Thank you. You may. (*offers her cheek*)

CECILY (*very sweetly*): I knew there must be some misunderstanding, Miss Fairfax. The gentleman whose arm is around your waist is my dear guardian, Mr. Jack Worthing.

GWENDOLEN: I beg your pardon?

CECILY: This is Uncle Jack.

GWENDOLEN (*falling back*): Jack! Oh!

(ALGERNON *enters.*)

CECILY: Here is Ernest.

ALGERNON (*going over to* CECILY *without seeing anyone else*): My own love! (*offers to kiss her*)

CECILY (*drawing back*): A moment, Ernest! May I ask you—are you to be married to this young lady?

ALGERNON (*looking round*): To what young lady? Good heavens! Do you mean Gwendolen!

CECILY: Yes! To good heavens, Gwendolen. I mean to Gwendolen.

ALGERNON (*laughing*): Of course not! What could have put such an idea into your pretty little head?

CECILY: Thank you. (*presenting her cheek to be kissed*) You may. (ALGERNON *kisses her.*)

GWENDOLEN: I felt there was some slight error, Miss Cardew. The gentleman who is now kissing you is my cousin, Mr. Algernon Moncrieff.

CECILY (*breaking away from Algernon*): Algernon Moncrieff! Oh! (*The two girls move towards each other and put their arms around each other's waists as if for protection.*)

CECILY: Are you called Algernon?

ALGERNON: I am.

CECILY: Oh!

GWENDOLEN: Is your name really Jack?

JACK: I could tell you no if I liked. I could tell you anything if I liked. However, my name is Jack. It has been Jack for years.

CECILY (*to* GWENDOLEN): We have both been the victims of a terrible fraud.

GWENDOLEN: My poor, wounded Cecily!

CECILY: My sweet, wronged Gwendolen!

GWENDOLEN (*slowly and seriously*): You will call me sister, will you not? (*They hug.* JACK *and* ALGERNON *groan and walk back and forth.*)

CECILY (*rather brightly*): There is just one question I would like to ask my guardian.

GWENDOLEN: A good idea! Mr. Worthing, there is just one question I would like to ask you. Where is your brother Ernest? We are both engaged to be married to your brother Ernest. It is a matter of importance to us to know where your brother Ernest is.

JACK (*slowly and uncertainly*): Gwendolen— Cecily—it is very painful for me to be forced to speak the truth. It is the first time in my life that I have been placed in such a painful position. I am not used to doing anything of the kind. However, I will tell you that I have no brother Ernest. I have no brother at all. I never had a brother in my life. I have not the smallest plan of ever having one in the future.

CECILY (*surprised*): No brother at all?

JACK (*cheerily*): None!

GWENDOLEN (*severely*): You never had a brother of any kind?

JACK (*pleasantly*): Never. Not even of any kind.

GWENDOLEN: I am afraid it is quite clear, Cecily, that neither of us is engaged to be married to anyone.

CECILY: It is not a very pleasant position for a young girl suddenly to find herself in.

GWENDOLEN: Let us go into the house. They will hardly come after us there.

CECILY: No, men are cowards, aren't they? (*They go into the house with scornful looks.*)

JACK (*coldly*): This awful state of things is what you call Bunburying, I guess?

ALGERNON: Yes, and a perfectly wonderful Bunbury it is. The most wonderful Bunbury I have had in my life.

JACK (*sharply*): Well, you have no right to Bunbury here.

ALGERNON: That is silly. One has a right to Bunbury anywhere one chooses. Every serious Bunburyist knows that.

JACK: Serious Bunburyist! Good heavens!

ALGERNON: Well, one must be serious about something, if one wants to be amused in life. I happen to be serious about Bunburying. What you are serious about I have no idea. About everything, I should think. Your interests are so unimportant. It is your nature.

JACK: Well, the only small satisfaction I have in all of this business is that your friend

Bunbury is done. You won't be able to run down to the country quite so often, dear Algy. A good thing it is, too.

ALGERNON: Your brother is a bit dead, isn't he, dear Jack? You won't be able to go to London so often. That wicked habit is ended. That is not a bad thing, either.

JACK: As for your manner toward Miss Cardew, I must say that there is no excuse for your taking in a sweet, simple, innocent girl like that.

ALGERNON: I can see no possible reason for your lying to a brilliant, clever, experienced young lady like Miss Fairfax. To say nothing of the fact that she is my cousin.

JACK: I wanted to marry Gwendolen, that is all. I love her.

ALGERNON: Well, I wanted to marry Cecily. I adore her.

JACK: There is no chance of your marrying Miss Cardew.

ALGERNON: I don't think there is much likelihood, Jack, of you and Miss Fairfax being married.

JACK: Well, that is no business of yours.

Algernon: If it were my business, I wouldn't talk about it. (*begins to eat muffins*) It is very rude to talk about one's business. Only people like stockbrokers do that. Even then they only do so at dinner parties.

(In this scene, ALGERNON *and* JACK *behave with carefully controlled greed. They eat as fast as they can, while trying to appear polite. Their behavior is similar to that of* CECILY *and* GWENDOLEN *at tea.)*

JACK: How you can sit there, calmly eating muffins when we are in this horrible trouble? I can't understand it. You seem heartless.

ALGERNON: Well, I can't eat muffins when I am upset. The butter might get on my cuffs. One should always eat muffins quite calmly. It is the only way to eat them.

JACK: I say it's heartless your eating muffins at all, right now.

ALGERNON: When I am in trouble, eating is the only thing that helps me. Indeed, when I am in really great trouble, I refuse everything except food and drink. Right now, I am eating muffins because I am unhappy. Besides, I am very fond of muffins. *(rising)*

JACK *(rising)*: Even so, you should not eat them all in that greedy way. *(takes muffins from* ALGERNON*)*

ALGERNON *(offering cake)*: I wish you would have cake instead. I don't like cake.

JACK: Well! I guess a man may eat his own muffins in his own garden.

ALGERNON: You have just said it was heartless to eat muffins.

JACK: I said it was heartless of you. That is very different.

ALGERNON: That may be. However, the muffins are the same. (*He takes the muffins from JACK.*)

JACK: Algy, I wish you would go.

ALGERNON: You can't ask me to go without dinner. I never go without my dinner. No one ever does, except vegetarians and people like that. Besides, I am to be christened by Dr. Chasuble at a quarter to six under the name of Ernest.

JACK: My dear fellow, the sooner you give up that nonsense the better. Dr. Chasuble will be christening me at 5:30 P.M. I will, of course, take the name of Ernest. Gwendolen wishes it. We can't both be christened Ernest. It's silly. Besides, I have a right to be christened if I like. There is no proof that I ever have been christened. I think it likely that I never was. So does Dr. Chasuble. It is different in your case. You have been christened already.

ALGERNON: Yes, but not for years.

JACK: Yes, but you *have* been christened. That is the important thing.

ALGERNON: Quite so. I know I can stand it. If you are not sure about having been christened, it is dangerous to try it now. You might become ill. You must remember that someone very close to you very nearly died in Paris from a severe chill.

JACK: Yes, but you said that severe chills did not run in families.

ALGERNON: I expect they do now. Science is always learning new things.

JACK (*picking up the muffin dish*): Oh, that is nonsense. You are always talking nonsense.

ALGERNON: Jack, you are at the muffins again! I wish you wouldn't. There are only two left. (*takes them*) I told you I was very fond of muffins.

JACK: I hate cake.

ALGERNON: Why then do you allow cake to be served to your guests? What a terrible host you are!

JACK: Algernon! I have already told you to go. I don't want you here. Why don't you go!

ALGERNON: I am not quite done with my tea, and there is still one muffin left. (JACK *groans and sinks into a chair.* ALGERNON *continues eating.*)

Curtain

Act 3

Living room at the Manor House. GWENDOLEN *and* CECILY *are at the window, looking out into the garden.*

GWENDOLEN: They did not follow us into the house as anyone else would have done. That shows me that they have some sense of shame left.

CECILY: They have been eating muffins. That looks like they are sorry.

GWENDOLEN (*after a pause*): They don't seem to notice us at all. Couldn't you cough?

(CECILY *coughs.*)

GWENDOLEN: They're looking at us. What nerve!

CECILY: They're coming closer. That's very bold of them.

GWENDOLEN: Let us keep silent.

CECILY: Yes. It's the only thing to do.

(JACK *enters, followed by* ALGERNON. *They whistle.*)

GWENDOLEN: This silence seems to lead to an unpleasant effect.

CECILY: A most displeasing one.

GWENDOLEN: We will not be the first to speak.

CECILY: Of course not.

GWENDOLEN: Mr. Worthing, I have something important to ask you.

CECILY (*to* GWENDOLEN): Gwendolen, your common sense is priceless. (*She turns to* ALGERNON) Mr. Moncrieff, please answer this question. Why did you pretend to be my guardian's brother?

ALGERNON: So that I might meet you.

CECILY (*to* GWENDOLEN): That seems a fine reason, does it not?

GWENDOLEN: Yes, dear, if you can believe him.

CECILY: I don't. However, I still admire the answer.

GWENDOLEN: True. In many matters, it is style, not sincerity, that is important. Mr. Worthing, why have you been pretending to have a brother? Was it so you could come to town to see me?

JACK: Do you doubt it, Miss Fairfax?

GWENDOLEN: I do have doubts, but I will crush them. This is no time for doubt. (*moving to* CECILY) Their answers seem fine. I like Mr. Worthing's answer. It has the stamp of truth.

CECILY: I am happy with what Mr. Moncrieff said. His voice alone helps one believe him.

GWENDOLEN: Should we forgive them?

CECILY: Yes. I mean no.

GWENDOLEN: True! I had forgotten. There are principles here that one cannot give up. Which of us should tell them?

74

CECILY: Could we speak at the same time?

GWENDOLEN: An excellent idea! I always speak at the same time as other people. I will keep the beat. Will you follow me?

CECILY: Of course. (GWENDOLEN *beats time with uplifted finger.*)

GWENDOLEN *and* CECILY (*speaking together*): Your first names are still an impossible problem.

JACK *and* ALGERNON (*speaking together*): Our first names! Is that all? We are going to be christened this afternoon and change them.

GWENDOLEN (*to* JACK): You would do this terrible thing for me?

JACK: I would.

CECILY (*to* ALGERNON): To please me, you would face this fearful trial?

ALGERNON: I would.

GWENDOLEN: How silly to say that women are the equal of men! Where courage is involved, men are far beyond us.

JACK: We are. (*clasps hands with* ALGERNON)

CECILY: They have times of bravery that we women know nothing about.

GWENDOLEN (*to* JACK): Darling!

ALGERNON (*to* CECILY): Darling! (*The two couples fall into each other's arms.*)

(MERRIMAN *enters. When he does, he coughs loudly to tell that he is coming.*)

MERRIMAN: Ahem! Ahem! Lady Bracknell!

JACK: Good heavens!

(LADY BRACKNELL *enters. The couples separate in alarm.* MERRIMAN *leaves.*)

LADY BRACKNELL (*severely*): Gwendolen! What does this mean?

GWENDOLEN: Only that I am to be married to Mr. Worthing, Mamma.

LADY BRACKNELL (*speaking with an air of command*): Come here. Sit down. (*turns to* JACK) I used a small coin to buy information from a servant about where my daughter went. Then, I followed her here. Her father thinks she is attending a lecture. I do not plan to tell him the truth. Indeed, I have never told him the truth on any question. I think that would be wrong. You do understand that you must not see my daughter any longer. On this point, I am firm.

JACK (*bravely*): I am to be married to Gwendolen!

LADY BRACKNELL: You are not, sir. Now, to Algernon.

ALGERNON: Yes, Aunt Augusta?

LADY BRACKNELL: Is this where your ill friend Mr. Bunbury lives?

ALGERNON (*stumbling over his words*): Oh! No! Bunbury doesn't live here. Bunbury is somewhere else. In fact, Bunbury is dead.

LADY BRACKNELL: Dead! When did Mr. Bunbury die? His death must have been very sudden.

ALGERNON (*airily*): Oh! I killed Bunbury this afternoon. I mean he died this afternoon.

LADY BRACKNELL: What did he die of?

ALGERNON: Bunbury? Oh, he blew up.

LADY BRACKNELL: Blew up!

ALGERNON: My dear Aunt Augusta, I mean he was found out! The doctors found out that Bunbury could not live. So, Bunbury died.

LADY BRACKNELL: He seems to have had great belief in his doctors. I am glad he followed their advice. Now that we are rid of this Mr. Bunbury, I have a question.
Mr. Worthing, who is that young person whose hand my nephew Algernon is holding in that strange manner?

JACK: That lady is Miss Cecily Cardew, my ward. (LADY BRACKNELL *bows coldly to* CECILY.)

ALGERNON (*quietly*): I am to be married to Cecily, Aunt Augusta.

LADY BRACKNELL: I beg your pardon?

CECILY: Mr. Moncrieff and I are engaged to be married, Lady Bracknell.

LADY BRACKNELL (*with a shiver, crossing to the sofa and sitting down*): I do not know if there is something in the air of this part of England. However, the number of engagements seems far above average.

I think some questions are called.for
Mr. Worthing, is Miss Cardew at all
connected with any of the larger railway
stations in London? Until yesterday, I had
no idea that there were any families that
came from a railway station. (JACK *looks
furious but controls himself.*)

JACK (*in a clear, cold voice*): Miss Cardew is the
granddaughter of the late Mr. Thomas
Cardew of 149 Belgrave Square, S.W. He
also had homes at Gervase Park, Dorking,
Surrey; and the Sporran, Fifeshire, N.B.

LADY BRACKNELL: That is fine. Three addresses
always sound good. Are they real?

JACK: I have the guides to royalty of the time.
You may look at them, Lady Bracknell.

LADY BRACKNELL (*grimly*): I have known strange
errors in the guides.

JACK: Miss Cardew's family lawyers are
Messrs. Markby, Markby, and Markby.

LADY BRACKNELL: Markby, Markby, and Markby?
A firm of the very highest sort. I am told
that one of the Mr. Markbys may be seen
at dinner parties. So far, I am satisfied.

JACK (*very irritable*): How very kind of you,
Lady Bracknell! I have also certificates
of Miss Cardew's birth, baptism, whooping
cough, registration, vaccination,
confirmation, and the measles, both the
German and the English variety.

LADY BRACKNELL: Ah! A life full of events, I see.
Perhaps it is too exciting for a young girl.
I am not in favor of early experience. *(rises,
looks at her watch)* Gwendolen! The time is
near for us to leave. Before we go,
Mr. Worthing, I should ask you if
Miss Cardew has any fortune.

JACK *(casually)*: Oh, Mr. Cardew left her a very
large fortune. That is all. Good-bye, Lady
Bracknell. So pleased to have seen you.

LADY BRACKNELL *(sitting down again)*: A moment,
Mr. Worthing. A very large fortune!
Miss Cardew seems most attractive, now
that I look at her. Few girls today have any
of the qualities that last and get better with
time. *(to* CECILY*)* Come over here, dear.
(CECILY *goes across.*) Pretty child! Your
dress is sadly simple. You hair looks as
nature might have left it. I am sure we can
change all that. A French maid creates
marvelous results in no time. I remember
suggesting one to young Lady Lancing. After
three months, her own husband did not
know her.

JACK *(aside)*: After six months, nobody did.

LADY BRACKNELL *(glares at* JACK *for a few
moments. Then she bends, with a smile, to*
CECILY.*)*: Kindly turn, sweet child. (CECILY
turns around.) No, the side view is what I
want. (CECILY *shows her profile.*) Yes, as I
thought. A good profile. The two troubles

79

of our age are no principles and no profiles. The chin a little higher, dear. Style depends on the way the chin is worn. They are worn very high, right now. Algernon!

ALGERNON: Yes, Aunt Augusta!

LADY BRACKNELL: There are social possibilities in Miss Cardew's profile.

ALGERNON: Cecily is the sweetest, dearest, prettiest girl in the whole world. I don't care at all about social possibilities.

LADY BRACKNELL: Never speak ill of Society, Algernon. Only people who can't get into it do that. (*to* CECILY) Dear child, of course you know that Algernon has only his debts to depend upon. I do not approve of marriages based on money. When I married Lord Bracknell, I had no fortune. However, I never dreamed of letting that stand in my way. Well, I suppose I must give my approval.

ALGERNON: Thank you, Aunt Augusta.

LADY BRACKNELL (*graciously*): Cecily, you may kiss me!

CECILY (*kisses her*): Thank you, Lady Bracknell.

LADY BRACKNELL: You may also call me Aunt Augusta.

CECILY: Thank you, Aunt Augusta.

LADY BRACKNELL: The marriage should take place quite soon.

ALGERNON: Thank you, Aunt Augusta.

CECILY: Thank you, Aunt Augusta.

LADY BRACKNELL: I am not in favor of long engagements. They give people the chance to find out about each other before marriage. That is never a good idea.

JACK: Excuse me, Lady Bracknell. This engagement is out of the question. I am Miss Cardew's guardian. She cannot marry without my consent until she comes of age. That consent I will not give.

LADY BRACKNELL: Why, may I ask? Algernon is a very available young man. He has nothing, but he looks as if he has everything. What more can one want?

JACK: I am sorry to have to tell you this, Lady Bracknell. The fact is that I do not like his character. I think he is untruthful. (ALGERNON *and* CECILY *look at him in amazement.*)

LADY BRACKNELL: My nephew Algernon? Impossible! He is a graduate of Oxford University.

JACK: I fear there is no doubt. This afternoon, I took a short trip to London. He entered my house by pretending to be my brother. Then, during the afternoon, he captured the affection of Cecily. He later stayed to tea and ate every muffin. All the time, he knew that I have no brother. I never had a brother. I don't intend to have a brother, not of any kind. I told him so myself.

LADY BRACKNELL: Well! Mr. Worthing, after thinking it over, I have decided to overlook my nephew's conduct toward you.

JACK: That is very generous of you, Lady Bracknell. My own decision, however, cannot be changed. I will not give my approval.

LADY BRACKNELL (*to* CECILY): Come here, sweet child. (CECILY *goes over.*) How old are you, dear?

CECILY: Well, I am really only 18, but I always say I am 20 when I go to evening parties.

LADY BRACKNELL: You are perfectly right in that. No woman should be exact about her age. It looks so planned. (*thoughtfully*) Eighteen, but 20 at evening parties. Well, it will not be long before you are of age and free from your guardian. His approval is not, after all, important.

JACK: Please excuse me, Lady Bracknell. It is only fair to tell you that based on her grandfather's will, Miss Cardew is not of age till she is 35.

LADY BRACKNELL: That is not a big problem. Thirty-five is a lovely age. London is full of women of the very highest birth who have been 35 for years. Lady Dumbleton is one. She has been 35 since she became 40. That was many years ago. Cecily will be even lovelier at that age than right now. Also, her property will be worth more.

CECILY: Algy, could you wait till I was 35?

ALGERNON: Of course, Cecily. You know I could.

CECILY: Yes, I thought so. However, I couldn't wait that long. I hate waiting even five minutes for anybody. It makes me rather cross. I am not always on time, I know, but I do like others to be. Waiting is not possible.

ALGERNON: Then, what is to be done, Cecily?

CECILY: I don't know, Mr. Moncrieff.

LADY BRACKNELL: Miss Cardew says she cannot wait till she is 35. I beg you to think again.

JACK: My dear Lady Bracknell, the matter is in your hands. When you agree to my marriage with Gwendolen, I will allow your nephew to marry Cecily.

LADY BRACKNELL (*rising and drawing herself up*): What you ask is not possible.

JACK: Then, a loving friendship is all any of us can look forward to.

LADY BRACKNELL: That is not what I plan for Gwendolen. Algernon, of course, can choose for himself. (*pulls out her watch*) Come, dear. (GWENDOLEN *rises.*) We have already missed five, if not six, trains. People will talk about us.

(CANON CHASUBLE *enters.*)

CANON CHASUBLE: We are ready for
the christenings.

LADY BRACKNELL: The christenings, sir! It is
somewhat early for that.

CANON CHASUBLE (*looking rather puzzled and
pointing to* JACK *and* ALGERNON): Both these
gentlemen have said they wanted to be
baptized.

LADY BRACKNELL: At their ages? The idea is
wrong. Algernon, I will not hear of such
a thing. Lord Bracknell would be displeased
if he learned that you wasted your time and
money in this way.

CANON CHASUBLE: Then, there are to be no
christenings at all this afternoon?

JACK: I don't think that, right now, it would be
of much use to either of us, Dr. Chasuble.

CANON CHASUBLE: I am sad to hear this from
you, Mr. Worthing. I will return to the
church at once. I have just been told that
Miss Prism has been waiting for me there.

LADY BRACKNELL: Miss Prism! Did you say
Miss Prism?

CANON CHASUBLE: Yes, Lady Bracknell. I am on
my way to join her.

LADY BRACKNELL: Please let me keep you for
a moment. This matter may be of deep
importance to Lord Bracknell and myself.
Is this Miss Prism a female of unpleasant

appearance, having something to do with education?

CANON CHASUBLE (*somewhat indignantly*): She is a true lady. The very picture of respectability.

LADY BRACKNELL: It is the same person. What position does she hold in your household?

CANON CHASUBLE (*severely*): I am not married.

JACK (*breaking in*): For the last three years, Miss Prism has been Miss Cardew's governess.

LADY BRACKNELL: I must see her. Send for her.

CANON CHASUBLE (*looking off*): She approaches. She is nearly here.

(MISS PRISM *enters in a hurry.*)

MISS PRISM: I was told you expected me at the church, dear Canon. I have been waiting for you there for an hour and 45 minutes. (*catches sight of* LADY BRACKNELL *who is giving her a stony glare.* MISS PRISM *grows pale and trembles. She looks as if she would like to escape.*)

LADY BRACKNELL (*in a severe voice*): Prism! (MISS PRISM *bows her head in shame.*) Come here, Prism! (MISS PRISM *comes close in a humble manner.*) Prism! Where is that baby? (*General alarm.* CANON CHASUBLE *starts back in horror.* ALGERNON *and* JACK *pretend to shield* CECILY *and* GWENDOLEN *from the details of a terrible scandal.*) Twenty-eight years ago, Prism, you left Lord Bracknell's house.

You had a baby carriage. That carriage had within it a baby boy. You never came back. A few weeks later, the police found the carriage at midnight. It was by itself in a corner of Bayswater. It had only the pages of a longer romantic novel that was more sickening than usual. (MISS PRISM *starts in anger.*) The baby was not there! (*Everyone looks at* MISS PRISM.) Prism! Where is that baby? (*a pause*)

MISS PRISM: Lady Bracknell, I do not know. I only wish that I did. The facts of the case are these: That day will be forever in my memory. As usual, I planned to take the baby out. I had also with me an old, but large, handbag. I had planned to place in the handbag a work of fiction written in my few free hours. Then, my mind wandered, for which I never can forgive myself. I put the novel in the carriage and the baby in the handbag.

JACK (*who has been listening closely*): Where did you put the handbag?

MISS PRISM: Do not ask me, Mr. Worthing.

JACK: Miss Prism, this is a very important matter to me. I must know where you put the handbag.

MISS PRISM: I left it in the coat room of a large railway station.

JACK: What railway station?

MISS PRISM (*quite crushed*): Victoria. The Brighton line. (*sinks into a chair*)

JACK: I must go to my room for a moment. Gwendolen, wait here for me.

GWENDOLEN: If you are not too long, I will wait here for you all my life.

(JACK *goes off to the left in great excitement.*)

CANON CHASUBLE: What does this mean, Lady Bracknell?

LADY BRACKNELL: I dare not guess. In good families this sort of thing is not supposed to happen. It is not thought to be right. (*Noises heard overhead as if someone were throwing trunks about. Everyone looks up.*)

CECILY: Uncle Jack seems excited.

CANON CHASUBLE: He is very emotional.

LADY BRACKNELL: This noise is very unpleasant. It sounds as if he were having an argument. I do not like arguments of any kind. They are always rude.

CANON CHASUBLE (*looking up*): It has stopped now. (*The noise grows louder.*)

LADY BRACKNELL: I wish he would finish.

GWENDOLEN: The suspense is terrible. I hope it will last.

(JACK *enters with a black leather handbag in his hand.*)

JACK (*rushing over to* MISS PRISM): Is this the handbag, Miss Prism? Look at it carefully

before you speak. The happiness of more than one life depends on your answer.

MISS PRISM (*calmly*): It seems to be mine. Yes, here is the damage from the bus accident. Here is the stain on the lining caused by an exploding drink. Here, on the lock, are my initials. The bag is mine. I am happy to have it returned to me. It has been a bother being without it all these years.

JACK (*in a pathetic voice*): Miss Prism, I was the baby you placed in it.

MISS PRISM (*amazed*): You?

JACK (*hugging her*): Yes . . . mother!

MISS PRISM (*drawing back in offense*): Mr. Worthing! I am unmarried!

JACK: Unmarried! This a serious blow. However, who has the right to disapprove? Why should there be one law for men and another for women? Mother, I forgive you. (*He tries to hug her again.*)

MISS PRISM (*still more displeased*): Mr. Worthing, there is some mistake. (*pointing to* LADY BRACKNELL) There is the lady who can tell you who you really are.

JACK (*after a pause*): Lady Bracknell, I hate to seem curious. However, would you please tell me who I am?

LADY BRACKNELL: The news will not please you. You are the son of my poor sister, Mrs. Moncrieff. You are Algernon's elder brother.

JACK (*in great excitement*): Algy's elder brother! Then, I have a brother after all. I knew I had a brother! I always said I had a brother! (*grabs* ALGERNON) Algy, you rascal, you will have to treat me with respect. You have never behaved to me like a brother in all your life.

ALGERNON: Well, not till today, I must say. (*shakes hands with* JACK)

GWENDOLEN (*to* JACK): My own! Yet, what own are you? What is your first name, now that you are someone else?

JACK: I had quite forgotten about that. Your decision about my name is final?

GWENDOLEN: I never change, except in my affections.

CECILY: What a fine nature you have, Gwendolen!

JACK: Then, the question had better be cleared up at once. Aunt Augusta, just a moment. When Miss Prism left me in the handbag, had I been christened?

LADY BRACKNELL: Your fond parents gave you every luxury money could buy—including christening.

JACK: Then, I was christened! That is settled.

Now, what name was I given? Let me know the worst.

LADY BRACKNELL: Being the eldest son you were naturally christened after your father.

JACK: Yes, but what was my father's first name?

LADY BRACKNELL (*thoughtfully*): I cannot recall the general's first name. I am sure he had one. He was a bit odd in his later years. That was the result of the Indian climate and marriage and other things of that kind.

JACK: Algy! Can't you remember what our father's first name was?

ALGERNON: My dear boy, we were never even on speaking terms. He died before I was a year old.

JACK: His name would be in the Army Lists of that time?

LADY BRACKNELL: The general was a man of peace, except in his home life. I am sure his name would appear in any military directory.

JACK: The Army Lists of the last 40 years are here. These records should have been my only study. (*rushes to the bookcase and tears the books out*) M. Generals . . . Mallam, Maxbohm, Magley, what terrible names they have—Markby, Migsby, Mobbs, Moncrieff! First names, Ernest John. (*puts book very quietly down and speaks quite calmly*) I always said, Gwendolen, my name was Ernest, didn't I? Well, it is Ernest.

LADY BRACKNELL: Yes, I remember now that the general was called Ernest. I knew I had some reason to dislike the name.

GWENDOLEN: Ernest! My own Ernest! I felt from the first that you have no other name!

JACK: Gwendolen, it is a terrible thing for a man to find out that all his life he has been speaking the truth. Can you forgive me?

GWENDOLEN (*thoughtfully*): I can. For I feel that you are sure to change.

JACK: My own one!

CANON CHASUBLE (*to* MISS PRISM): My happiness! (*hugs her*)

MISS PRISM (*with enthusiasm*): Frederick! At last!

ALGERNON: Cecily! (*hugs her*) At last!

JACK: Gwendolen! (*hugs her*) At last!

LADY BRACKNELL: My nephew, you seem to be showing a lack of seriousness.

JACK: Oh no, Aunt Augusta. I now see for the first time in my life the Importance of Being Earnest.

Curtain